The evening sun in the Imjin River.

HEADQUARTERS, UNITED NATIONS COMMAND
APO SAN FRANCISCO 96301

PAJ-PI   1 April 1985

MAJOR WAYNE KIRKBRIDE
19th Support Command
APO 96212-0171

SUBJECT: The Book "Panmunjom" Written by Major Wayne Kirkbride

1. Reference your request of 5 March 1985 for security review of your proposed book, "Panmunjom." This publication has been reviewed and there is no objection to publication by Hollym Corporation.

2. You have been provided a copy of recommended changes from the Commander, United Nations Command Support Group-Joint Security Area. Those changes that are factual in nature should be incorporated into your manuscript. Those that are solely on style are for your consideration.

3. Any questions in this regard should be referred to my office, ATTN: Public Information Division, TEL (293-3290).

THEODORE R. HEIL
Colonel, USAF
Director of Public Affairs

〈판문점 유엔군사령부 검열필〉

First published in February 1985
Enlarged edition in 1993
Fourth printing, 1994
by Hollym International Corp.
18 Donald Place
Elizabeth, New Jersey 07208 USA
Phone: (908)353-1655 Fax: (908)353-0255

Published simultaneously in Korea
by Hollym Corporation; Publishers
14-5 Kwanchol-dong, Chongno-gu, Seoul 110-111, Korea
Phone: (02)735-7554 Fax: (02)730-5149

ISBN: 0-930878-42-6
Library of Congress Catalog Card Number: 85-80491

Printed in Korea

CONTENTS:

PHOTO CREDITS:

US Army photos by Mr. Ray Ueno pages 3, 21, 22, 27, 29, 32, 34, 37, 44, 48, 49, 50, 51, 52, 53, 54.
US Army photos by other photographers 62, 69, 70, 71, 72, 73, 74, 75, 76, 77, 78, 79, 80.
Hollym photos all others.

ACKNOWLEDGEMENTS:

Thanks to Commander, United Nations Command Security Force—Joint Security Area and to the USFK/EUSA/UNC Director of Public Affairs.

Part A. Mr. Ray Ueno, 1st Signal Brigade and owner of Professional Photographic Service Limited provided many of the photographs of the DMZ area. His photos have appeared in unofficial US Army publications such as *Korus* Magazine.

Part B. Reprinted with permission from *A Panorama of 5,000 Years: Korean History* by Andrew C. Nahm, Hollym International Corp.

Part C. Reprinted with permission from *DMZ: A Story of the Panmunjom Axe Murder* by Major Wayne A. Kirkbride, Hollym International Corp.

Hollym International Corp. skillfully assisted in providing necessary assistance to publish this Guide to Panmunjom. Other books by Hollym about Korea are: *A Guide to Korean Literature, Folk Tales from Korea, Korea's Cultural Roots,* and *The Yobo.*

The Road to Panmunjom

PREFACE

Panmunjom. The focus of the world has drifted to and from this former small farming town through the years. The traditional invasion route to Seoul has caused Chinese warriors, Japanese Samurai, Mongols and Manchus to travel through this area. During the Korean War a parachute operation was conducted at Munsan-ni, not far from Panmunjom. The area to the north was part of the operational area for the Hwanghae-do guerrillas who waged an unconventional war against the communists during and for a few years after the Korean War. Panmunjom is the site of the Armistice which ended the fighting of the Korean War.

Since the signing of the Armistice, Panmunjom has been the location where north meets south to resolve military, economic, and political problems. Red Cross representatives, Olympic officials, economic advisors as well as military negotiators have convened meetings at Panmunjom in an attempt to keep the peace and reunite the peninsula.

Over 75,000 visit Panmunjom each year to get an eye witness view of this important area.

My prayer is that this guide will become a resource for future historians to study about what Korea was like when it was a divided nation and that peaceful reunification will occur soon.

This rusted locomotive is forever stranded in the DMZ.

IN FRONT OF THEM ALL

The United Nations Command Security Force—Joint Security Area (UNCSF—JSA) is the unit tasked to provide all logistical support and security to all United Nations Command personnel working in the Joint Security Area, commonly referred to as Panmunjom. These men who stand face to face with the communist North Korean guards are also the tour guides for all visitors in the area.

Since its activation on 5 May 1952 the Security Force has been involved in many politically sensitive missions. On 20 July 1954 the unit was awarded the Meritorious Unit Citation for its outstanding service in support of the following operations:

— OPERATION BIG SWITCH - Return of 12,760 prisoners of war including 3,579 American.

— The Movement of the Custodial Forces India - Movement of 6,143 personnel from Inchon Port to the Demilitarized Zone by helicopter.

— OPERATION COMEBACK - Release by Custodial Forces, India of 23,000 anti-communist Chinese and North Koreans who refused to be repatriated.

— OPERATION RAINBOW - Repatriation from North Korea of the displaced persons and refugees.

In recent years the Security Force has been involved in the following actions:

— OPERATION BREECHES BUOY - Return of the crew of the *U.S.S. Pueblo* on 23 December 1968.

— OPERATION TEMPLE BELL - Return of an OH-23 helicopter crew in December 1969.

— OPERATION RUNAWAY I - Repatriation of 39 South Korean National civilian passengers of the hijacked Korean Air Lines aircraft on 14 February 1970.

— OPERATION PAUL BUNYAN - Trimming of a tree in the JSA on 21 August 1976 caused by the death of two UNC officers.

Two defections in the 1980's have focused world attention on Panmunjom. On 30 October 1981 a Czechoslovakian Neutral Nations Supervisory Commission member walked across the Military Demarcation Line and surrendered himself to UNC soldiers and requested asylum in the United States. On 23 November 1984 an interpreter at the Soviet Embassy in Pyongyang broke away from a tour and sprinted the entire 69 foot length of the corridor between the MAC Conference Building and the UNC Joint Duty Office to two UNC guards routinely stationed at the building. Seven North Korean guards chased the Soviet defector across the MDL and began firing at him. The quick thinking and return of fire by the two UNC guards, Pvt 2 Michael A. Burgoyne and PFC Jang Myung Ki saved the life of the defector but cost PFC Jang his life. Pvt Burgoyne was wounded and received the Purple Heart. Three North Korean guards were killed. The hero of this action was PFC Jang who was posthumously promoted to corporal, was awarded the Bronze Star with "V" device, and had a newly constructed building at Camp Bonifas dedicated in his honor.

The UNCSF—JSA will continue to carry out its vital mission and as long as the United Nations Command Military Armistice Commission exists, the soldiers of the JSA will continue to live up to their motto:

"IN FRONT OF THEM ALL"

FROM SEOUL TO PANMUNJOM

Today's traveler can make the trip to Panmunjom in less than one and one half hours. Major General William Dean reached Panmunjom in 1953 after evading the communists for 40 days and 3 year imprisonment as a prisoner of war. His travel took him as far north as Manchuria before he was repatriated at Panmunjom. Today's traveler will also travel in far better conditions than did General Dean or any of the prisoners of war.

The armor obstacles, army compounds, and increased guards that greet the traveler give a hint of the tense situation in this part of the world and indicate the possibility for war to break out at any time. However, since 27 July 1953 the traveler has found a countryside in peace, albeit a shaky peace. A ride to Panmunjom is a good time to reflect upon the fact that each Republic of Korea or United States soldier, airman, sailor, marine or civilian has maintained that peace through his or her professional service.

Unification Road from Seoul to Panmunjom.

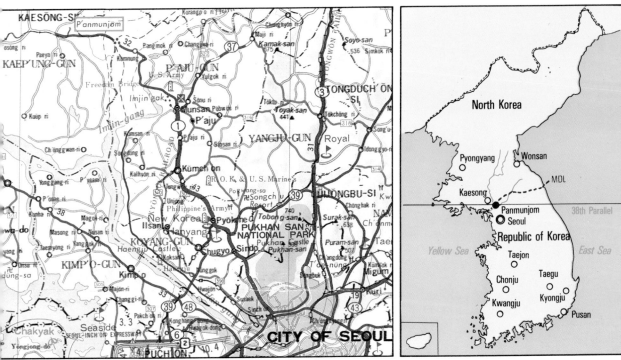

Top: Route map of Unification Road and Freedom Road.
Bottom: The Unification Observatory on Freedom Road.

Top: Memorial Monument to Republic of Philippine soldiers. The Republic of the Philippines sent 7,420 solsiders into battle less than three months after North Korean invaded the Republic of Korea. This is the first monument the traveler will view on the road to Panmunjom.
Bottom: Gloucester Valley Battle Monument of British Forces.

Just south of the village of Musan-ri is Unification Park. Three of the most famous memorials in this park are the War Correspondents Monument (top right) which is dedicated to 18 journalists killed while covering the Korean War, Marine Corps Monument for the Defence of Capital Area (top left), and the Loyal Monument for the Late Ten Human-bomb Heroes (bottom) which honors ten brave men from the ROK 1st Infantry Division who exploded bombs against their unprotected bodies to allow follow-on soldiers to accomplish their mission.

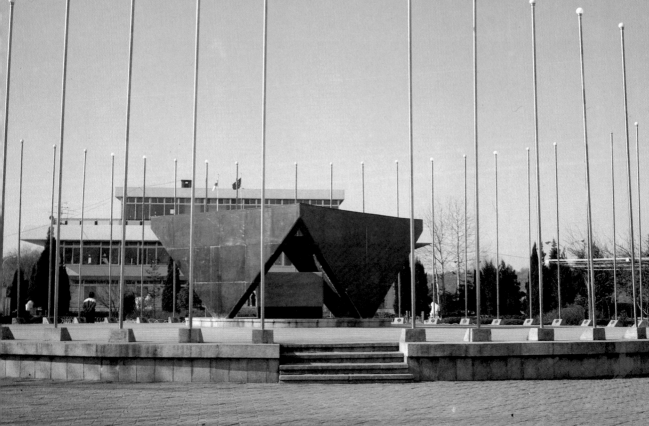

Pigeons strolling about near the Freedom Bridge (top left), Eternal Flame of Peace (top right), Monument to the Strategic Battlefield along the Imjin River (bottom right) and Memorial Monument to the U.S. for providing combat forces during the Korean War.

Three important monuments vicinity of Freedom Bridge. The 2nd U.S. Infantry Division fought during the Korean War (top left). President Harry S. Truman committed U.S. combat forces to Korea (top right), the Relaxation Plaza (bottom) allows tourists to sit and appreciate the park.

Top: The Anti-communism Exhibition Hall which displays war documents, captured infiltration equipment and weapons, a model of the 3rd Infiltration Tunnel, and other acts of aggression by the communists.
Bottom: Imjin-gak Restaurant.

Opposite: Monument in memory of the 17 Korean officials killed in the Rangoon Bombing of 9 October 1983. The bomb planted in Burma by the North Koreans narrowly missed the Republic of Korea President Chun Doo Hwan while he was on an official visit to that country.

Some of the weapons used during the Korean War.

TRAIN IS ANXIOUS TO RUN NORTH

This train once was able to begin a trip in Pusan on the southern tip of Korea and travel north to the Yalu River and on to Peking, China. Today this train is halted just shy of the Imjin River waiting for the peninsula to be reunited. This train, which is pointed north, seems to say to all who pass by that it wants "Peace to the North" so that it can run its course again.

FREEDOM BRIDGE

The two photos on the opposite page are the only photos permitted of the Freedom Bridge. This one lane bridge which spans the Imjin River is a strategic bridge and photographs are not allowed for security reasons. The renovation of the current bridge was completed on 10 Dec.1970 by the 109th RQK Engineer Battalion. However, piers from the former link between Munsan and North Korea still stand north of the Freedom Bridge in the Imjin River. The Freedom Bridge is now guarded by soldiers of the 1st Battalion 9th Infantry (Manchu) who proudly salute with their motto "KEEP UP THE FIRE." The opposite top photo explains the Freedom Bridge with an emphasis on the fact that 12,773 prisoners of war crossed the bridge after the Korean War. Only a limited number of Republic of Korea citizens are permitted to cross the Imjin River. For the others the Imjin-gak area is as close to Panmunjom as they will ever travel.

Train halted south of the Imjin River.

This is Imjin-gak park, the north-
ernmost that's accessible without
a special pass. It's possible only
by permission to cross Freedom
Bridge which stretches, in this
picture, from left to central part
of it.
Bottom: The southern end of the
remains of a highway bridge.
This still stands at the southern
end of Freedom Bridge (not seen
in this picture).

Top: Distant view of Seoul seen from the Unification Road. Seoul Tower is seen afar.
Bottom: Mangbaedan (Worshiping from - Afar Altar). Dispersed family members who left their hometowns in North Korea are conducting the ancestral rites looking toward the north, praying for unification.
Opposite: Milepost for North Korea. Although tourists can see the milepost, they can't go to the places it represents.

Opposite: The road to Panmunjom.

In front of them all.

CAMP BONIFAS

Camp Bonifas is the base camp for the United Nations Command Security Force—Joint Security Area. It is located 400 meters south of the southern boundary of the Demilitarized Zone. The tourists receive a detailed briefing in Ballinger Hall prior to visiting the JSA, eat in the NCO club, and have an opportunity to sign a guest book and purchase souvenirs in The Monastery, which is the home of the "Merry Mad Monks of the DMZ" ("The merriest monk of all" is that officer next to leave the unit).

This is home for the soldiers who support the Military Armistice Commission at JSA. Barracks, officers' quarters, a club, a swimming pool, a library, and other facilities have been recently constructed or are planned for the future.

Camp Bonifas was attacked by the North Koreans on August 29, 1967 in a raid which re-

sulted in one U.S. and two ROK soldiers killed and a total of 24 wounded.

JOINT SECURITY AREA

On 24 June 1951 North Korea, through the Soviet Ambassador to the UN, recommended a truce line be formed on the 38th Parallel. At this time the UNC forces were dug-in 50 miles north of the 38th Parallel. After an exchange of counter-offers the talks began at Kaesong and were later moved to the neutral site at Panmunjom. The village of Panmunjom was destroyed during the Korean War. In order to negotiate the Armistice a tent city was constructed. In the years that followed each side constructed its own buildings in the JSA and today there are 24 buildings in the area which is approximately 800 meters in diameter. JSA houses the Advance Secretariat of the UNCMAC and various offices and conference rooms.

A Joint Duty Office representative from each side is required to remain at the JSA 24 hours daily in order to rapidly respond to any incident.

The JSA straddles the Military Demarcation Line. In fact the MDL passes through the center of the negotiating table in the Military Armistice Commission Building. The 4 KPA guard posts south of the MDL were dismantled following the negotiations that occurred after the August 18, 1976 Panmunjom Axe Murder Incident.

This schematic of the vicinity of JSA is viewed from the north looking south. The yellow line dividing the schematic is the Military Demarcation Line (MDL). The MDL, marked by 1,291 yellow signs in English and Korean on one side and Korean and Chinese on the other side, stretches the 151 mile width of Korea from the East Sea or Sea of Japan on the east to the Han River in the west. Due east and adjacent to the JSA is the home of the Swiss and Swedish delegates to the Neutral Nations Supervisory Commission.

The JSA is the lower left concentration of buildings. The two entrances from the north cross the Sachon River via the Bridge of No Return and via the 72 Hour Bridge. Prior to the brutal Panmunjom Axe Murder Incident both forces had access to either side and the only entrance for the north was the Bridge of No Return. Subsequent agreements limited movement within the JSA and the northern forces could no longer enter the Republic of Korea. Therefore, another bridge was started and completed in 72 hours, hence its nickname. The roads which cross these two bridges meet in the north vicinity the building which is a replica of the site where the 1953 Armistice was signed.

The North Korean Propaganda Village and the Republic of Korea Freedom Village are south of the JSA and can be identified by their national flags.

The large curvature in the MDL in the top center of the schematic is the location of the 3rd Tunnel discovered in 1978.

Schematic diagram of the vicinity of JSA.   *Opposite: Gate to Camp Bonifas.*

Upper left: The Monastery "Home of the Merry Mad Monks of the DMZ.
Upper right: US Combined Forces Commander Powell inspecting the UNC volunteer units (Nov. 20, 1991).

Bottom: Memorial to remember those soldiers whose deeds made them "Forever in Front of Them All."

Upper left: JSA Bus at UNC Check point 2 which is on the south eastern flank of the JSA by the primary UNC access road from Camp Bonifas to the JSA.

Upper right: JSA Bus and ROK soldiers.
Bottom: Flag Plaza honoring the 16 nations which provided combat forces to the ROK during the Korean War

FREEDOM HOUSE

The Freedom House was designed, erected, and dedicated at Panmunjom by the people of the Republic of Korea with the support of the United Nations Command. This is a historical symbol of the hope for a peaceful reunification of the divided Korea under a free and democratic form of government. This serves as the forward administrative office for the ROK Red Cross. In the foreground is the Sunken Garden of the JSA.

The UNC sponsors approximately 75,000 tourists each year. A must for the visitors is a visit to the MAC Building and the Pagoda at the Freedom House. The Pagoda offers a bird's eye view of Panmunjom in several directions. The tense atmosphere becomes apparent when one views the JSA from this site.

Freedom House and Sunken Garden.

Central part of Panmunjom. On the left is located North Korea's Panmun-gak. On the right its counterpart, Republic of Korea's Freedom House and in the center is seen Conference Row.

PANMUN-GAK

The North Korean government sponsors about 9,000 tourists annually. It was on one such tour that a Soviet defector ran south to freedom in November 1984. Each visitor visits the Panmun-gak (right) which is the Joint Duty office of the North Korean Chinese Peoples Volunteers JSA.

Upper right: North Korean Panmun-gak. Bottom right: Preparing for Liberation Day ceremonies (Aug. 14, 1992). On Liberation Day, Aug. 15, 1992, hundreds of students from various schools including Kim Il-sung Univ. and Kim Chong-suk Teachers' College held a rally here. In the previous year, South Korean Park Song-hi, on an illegal visit to the North, also participated in the Panmun-gak ceremonies.

Below: Panmun-gak and North Korean guard posts.
Opposite bottom: Around UNC CP 5. This guard post which is located up the oval road also serves as tourists' observatory because it has the best view of the north. On the left is Bridge of No Return.

This is the north viewed from UNC CP 5. North Korea's War Museum is seen.

Upper left: UNC guard points out an object from Checkpoint 5.

Upper right: Prime Minister Thatcher of Great Britain and her entourage observing north from CP 5.

Bottom: Viewed from CP 5. The poplar stump from the Panmunjom Axe Murder Incident, Bridge of No Return, and North Korea's propaganda village and her flagpole there.

Upper left: Chancellor of Germany Helmut Kohl overlooks conference row from the Freedom House (Mar. 2, 1993).
Bottom left: North Korean students on Panmunjom tour. All are wearing Kim Il-sung badges on their left chest.

Upper right: Australian Prime Minister Keating with DMZ escorts at United Nations Command Checkpoint 3 (Jun. 22, 1993).
Bottom right: A view of North Korea from the JSA.

Military Armistice Commission Building.

The Military Armistice Commission (MAC) Building houses 4 levels of meetings essential to the upkeep of the 27 July 1953 Armistice Agreement. These meetings are conducted in an unfriendly and often hostile atmosphere. Greetings are not exchanged, much less handshakes.

The full scale MAC meeting is held to discuss major violations of the Armistice. As pictured the UNC has a 2 star naval flag officer as the Senior Member, two members from the ROK, one from the UK, and a fifth member designated on a rotational basis from among the nations still represented in the UNC (Canada, Thailand, Philippines). Four members from the north are from the North Korean People's Army and one officer is from the Chinese People's Volunteer Army. One of the North Korean generals serves as the Senior Member. The Senior Member is the only speaker for each side. The side calling the meeting makes the opening statement. The UNC statement is first given in English and then is consecutively translated into Korean and Chinese.

View of Conference Row.

The North Korean statement is first given in Korean and followed by English and Chinese.

The next lower level is the Secretary's Meeting which is held to discuss lesser violations of the Armistice. It follows the same format as the MAC Meeting, without the Chinese statement translation.

The third level is the Joint Duty Officer meeting which is held every day of the year at noon except for Sundays and holidays. These meetings are held to discuss pertinent administrative information vital to the MAC. Each side is required to have a JDO on duty in the JSA 24 hours a day.

The fourth level of meetings is the Security Officer's Meeting. This meeting can be called by either side at any time deemed appropriate to ease the tension between the two guard forces.

Other meetings have been held in the Joint Security Area between representatives of the two Koreas to include Red Cross, Olympic Committee, and intra-governmental dialogues.

Security Officer Meeting.

Military Armistice Commission Meeting

Upper left: The UNC guardhouse near Conference Row.
Upper right: UNC soldiers changing guard.
Bottom: An American guard and a Republic of Korea soldier.

UNC GUARDS

All UNC guards have spotless civilian and military records. The American soldier must meet above height, weight, and aptitude requirements. The Korean soldier serves his entire thirty month tour at Panmunjom. He must be taller and larger than the average ROK soldier, have a basic fluency in both written and spoken English, and must possess at least a first degree Blackbelt in any of the martial arts.

KOREAN PEOPLE'S ARMY GUARDS

Kim Il Sung, the Premier of north Korea, reportedly served as a major in the Soviet Army prior to ascending to power and modeled his army after the Soviet army. Note the Soviet style of uniform and the goose step march.

Right: North Korean guardhouse.
Bottom left: A North Korean guard.
Bottom right: North Korean soldiers marching at Panmunjom.

THE AXE MURDER INCIDENT

On 18 August 1976 this tree was made a symbol of oppression. For three days it stood as a challenge to freedom everywhere. A group of free men rose up and cut down that tree leaving only this stump to remind the world of the resolve of the United Nations Command to maintain peace in the Republic of Korea.

THE BRIDGE OF NO RETURN

The Bridge of No Return is the spot where all prisoners of war were repatriated after the end of the Korean War. The returning UNC prisoner stopped at the bridge while exchange lists were verified. Once repatriated he went straight to a tent city where he discarded the communist POW uniform, showered, received new uniforms, and received a meal of real food to include icecream. The crew of the *U.S.S. Pueblo* returned across this bridge. This remains the only ground link between Seoul and Pyongyang.

This was the primary entrance to the JSA by the North Koreans while each side had free access to the entire JSA. At that time UNC Check Point 3 was known as "the loneliest outpost in the world" as it is just meters from North Korea. In September 1976 it was decided that the JSA would no longer be completely neutral and that the only personnel authorized to cross the MDL would be from the Neutral Nations Supervisory Commission and the Military Armistice Commission.

The North Korean forces now enter from the North across a bridge constructed in 72 hours and known as the "72 Hour Bridge."

Bottom: The poplar stump of the Panmunjom Axe Murder Incident.
Opposite top: Yellow marker to indicate Military Demarcation Line and Bridge of No Return.
Opposite bottom: An overall view around Bridge of No Return from CP 5.

Bottom and opposite: US President Bill Clinton on the Bridge of No Return. He showed concern for the level of fortification on the North side and the grim sacrifice South Korea makes for democracy (Jul. 11, 1993).

MILITARY
DEMARCATION LINE

RESIDENTS OF THE DMZ

The only human inhabitants of the DMZ are the members of the Neutral Nations Supervisory Commission (NNSC) and the villagers of Taesong-dong. The North Korean Propaganda Village is merely a village in a caretaker status as discussing on page 49. The village of Taesong-dong or Freedom Village is adjacent to the Military Demarcation Line. Taesong-dong can be translated ''Attaining Success Town.'' The residents have elected to reside on their ancestral homes rather than relocate to a safer life in the south. The citizens live under very rigid conditions as they must be out of their fields and in their village by dark each day and must be at home and accounted for with their windows and doors secured by 11:00 o'clock each night. They are continually blasted with propaganda from loudspeakers at Propaganda Village. The UNCSF—JSA provides a security and civil affairs unit for TSD.

Left: The flag of Taesong-dong which stands approximately 100 meters high.
Bottom left: UNCSF—TSD Civil Affairs Platoon sign.
Bottom right: Headquarters Building, Taesong-dong Security Platoon.

Upper left: Entrance to Taesong-dong (TSD) adjacent to the road to Panmunjom. The TSD sign and checkpoint are seen.

Upper right: Road to Unification Garden Pagoda. Bottom: A panorama of Taesong-dong viewed from the north toward the south.

Upper left: Taesong-dong viewed from Unification Garden Pagoda (Palgakchong or Octagonal Pavilion).

Upper right: Unification Garden Pagoda at Taesong-dong.
Bottom: Close up view of Taesong-dong.

Upper left: A typical Taesong-dong home. *Bottom: Villagers are threshing rice on a vacant*
Upper right: Woodpiles heaped up by the inner *lot adjacent to the village co-op store.*
roads of the village.

The farmers of Taesong-dong farms 14 to 17 acres which compares to 2 to 4 acres for the farmer to the south.

Top: The front gate of TSD Primary School. Villagers are drying rice on the broad schoolyard.
Bottom: Despite the rigid conditions they live under, life can be quite normal for the citizens of Taesong-dong.

Top right: Ginseng is grown in the northern part of the DMZ.
Middle right: Observation point and a concrete blockade wall for shielding tanks in the northern part of DMZ.
Bottom left: North Korean soldiers repairing one of their observation cameras in the DMZ.
Bottom right: North Korean propaganda can be seen and heard all around here; on billboards, writings and through loud speakers.

Wildlife abounds in the DMZ.

A HAVEN FOR WILDLIFE

The 4,000 meter wide Demilitarized Zone is probably the most militarized zone in the world as it is mined, has obstacles to foot or vehicle movement, and is constantly patrolled. There are no humans in this area except for the residents of Taesong-dong, the delegates to NNSC, and the well armed soldiers who guard the border on foot patrol or from the guard posts. The fact that this is one of the least inhabited areas of the world enables wildlife to flourish. In fact, several endangered species such as the beautiful Manchurian Crane, have found a sanctuary within the DMZ. The Ringneck Pheasant and the variety of the ducks which abound would make this a sportsmen's paradise if hunting were allowed. In higher elevations than that of Panmunjom, the native Korean bear, wildcat, and deer reside. It is the militarization of this area that has created a safe haven for all wildlife as they very seldom find themselves

Manchurian cranes in the DMZ.

Old (top) and new entrance to the DMZ.
Bottom right: UNC soldiers on patrol.

as someone's supper and are protected from the industrial pollution that has threatened wildlife in more populated areas.

NORTH KOREAN PROPAGANDA VILLAGE

The North Korean village of Kijong-dong is also located in the DMZ. It has been called "Propaganda Village" for a number of reasons, first and foremost of which is the extensive loud speaker system which broadcasts to the citizens of Taesong-dong and to anyone who will listen the praises of Kim Il Sung, the great, god-like leader. These broadcasts are emitted 6 to 12 hours a day, mostly at night. A second reason is that this is a village with no citizens. Although 15 to 20 workers are present every day, they are nothing more than caretakers of this city as they raise and lower the flag and maintain the facilities.

View of Propaganda Village.

The flag pole at Propaganda Village is 160 meters high and flies a flag 30 meters long.

Upper left: A typical Taesong-dong home.
Upper right: Woodpiles heaped up by the inner
roads of the village.

Bottom: Villagers are threshing rice on a vacant
lot adjacent to the village co-op store.

The farmers of Taesong-dong farms 14 to 17 acres which compares to 2 to 4 acres for the farmer to the south.

Upper left: UNC soldiers participating in an athletic meet at TSD Primary School.
Upper right: UNC soldiers on patrol.
Bottom: UNC soldiers participating in Taekwondo classes taught by ROK guards assigned to the JSA. Each ROK guard must have a black belt in either Taekwondo or Judo.

Bottom left: President Bill Clinton talks to 2nd Lieutenant Cecil Clark as they look into North Korea's village of Chijong-dong from Observation Post Ouellette (Jul. 1, 1993).
Upper right: Republic of Korea DMZ military police
Bottom right:ROK and US soldiers on counter infiltration patrol inside the DMZ.

READY ON THE DMZ

The primary mission of the combat forces in the vicinity of Panmunjom is to deter war. Quick Reaction Forces, Guard Post Duty, and Ambush and Reconnaissance Patrols are every day words for these soldiers as these troops conduct these missions every day of the year.

These soldiers remain in a high state of readiness. The soldier's weapon, protective mask, and individual equipment must always be ready. His weapon must be zeroed. His vehicles must be operational and with a full load of fuel. If he does not know to shoot a Light Anti-Tank Weapon (LAW) when an alert is called, he has no time to learn prior to moving out. If he does not have a canteen, there is no time to get one. There is no time for anything but to receive a fast briefing on the mission and move out.

Some JSA soldiers are ready to move on minutes notice. This requires then to sleep in their uniforms, eat in their barracks, rather than in dining facilities, and stay together at all times. Other JSA soldiers are on other levels of readiness, but are never less than ready to move out.

The Manchus of the 1st Battalion 9th Infantry (Manchu) and the DMZ Battalion of the 2nd Infantry Division stay just as ready. These are the combat forces in the area and they have to be prepared to respond to any contingency. There is always an artillery battery at Firing Point 4P3 which stays ready to move to their howitzers and initiate firing within minutes.

The ROK 1st Infantry Division is on the left and right of the US battalions and prides itself on its vigilance, dedication, and professionalism. Except for Guard Post Collier and Ouellette, all Guard Posts in the area are manned by their soldiers.

These soldiers' dedication and professional conduct contribute toward maintaining peace on this peninsula. The price of freedom remains eternal vigilance.

Top: The price of freedom is eternal vigilance. Bottom: Camp Liberty Bell is the home of Company A 1st Battalion 9th Infantry (Manchu). It is adjacent to Camp Bonifas.

58

Historical Background

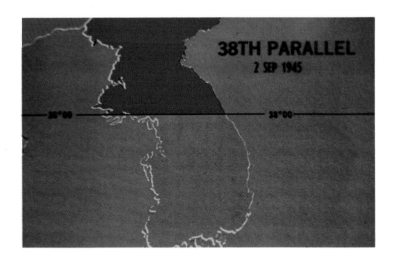

THE PARTITION AND FOREIGN OCCUPATION OF KOREA

The Cairo Declaration of December 1943 of the Allies (Great Britain, China and the United States) stated that Korea will be freed from Japan and she will be an independent nation "in due course." Although, U.S. President Franklin D. Roosevelt had a different plan for Korea, the Koreans interpreted the meaning of "in due course" as "when the Pacific War ended and the Japanese were removed from Korea." The Koreans were destined to taste a bitter cup with the U.S. plan to divide the Korean peninsula along the 38th parallel into two military operational zones of the U.S. and U.S.S.R., and occupy Korea. Moreover, it was not the plan of the U.S. to make Korea an independent nation im-mediately after her liberation from Japan. President Roosevelt wanted to put Korea under the trusteeship of the Allies for a considerable period (up to 35 years) of time after her liberation from Japan.

General John R. Hodge, Commander of U.S. forces in Korea, organized the United States Army Military Government and put South Korea under American military rule. The Koreans were disappointed and became angry, and the warm feelings of the Koreans toward the U.S. quickly cooled off.

The Republic of Korea, launched in a turbulent sea, weathered violent storms in its early stage. The first was the north Korean Communist-in-spired military insurrection of late 1948 and early 1949, and then the Korean War of 1950-53, which the North Korean Communists launched against

LIBERATION DAY, 15 AUG 1945

Top: People in Seoul rejoice at the news of Liberation on August 15, 1945.
Bottom:U.S. troops arrive at the Government General building.

the Republic in June 1950. These two tragic events determined the political character of the First Republic which lasted until April 1960.

THE KOREAN WAR

Despite the request made by the Korean government to the United States to keep its troops in Korea longer, the United States forces were withdrawn by late summer of 1949, leaving poorly trained and inadequately equipped Korean armed forces of 96,000 men to defend their national independence under some 500 American military advisers. The Soviet Union, on the other hand, gave a large amount of up-to-date military equipment, including 200 jet fighters and 500 heavy tanks, before it withdrew its troops from the north. South Korea had none of these. Moreover, some 2,500 Soviet military advisers remained in the north to train some 175,000 Communist troops there. By June 1950, the number of troops in the north grew to 200,000. With growing mili-

tary strength and supported by the Soviet Union, North Korea increased its threats to overthrow the Republic in the south.

On January 12, 1950, Secretary of State Dean Acheson disclosed in his speech given at the National Press Club in Washington, D.C. that South Korea was outside the U.S. defense perimeter which ran from the Aleutians to the Philippines via Japan. It was seen as a green signal by the north Korean Communists. On early Sunday, June 25, 1950, North Korean troops opened fire and launched a well planned war against South Korea.

North Korean troops, spearheaded by Soviet-made heavy tanks, crossed the 38th parallel, and within four days they captured the South Korean capital of Seoul and overran two-thirds of South Korea within a short period of time.

The North Korean attack prompted American President Harry S. Truman to send some American troops back to Korea from Japan, but they were unable to stop the advance of the invaders. Both South Korean and U. S. forces took

UN SECURITY COUNCIL, JUL 1950

a last stand in the Pusan region in the southeastern corner of the peninsula east of the Naktong River.

Realizing the grave danger to the existence of the Republic of Korea, President Truman requested the assistance of U.N. members for South Korea. The Security Council of the U.N. condemned North Korea as an aggressor and asked the member nations to provide military and other assistance to South Korea. The United States and 15 other nations joined the war to repel the aggressors and the United Nations forces were organized.

An American general, Douglas MacArthur, Supreme Commander of the Allied Forces in the Pacific (SCAP), was named Commander of the U.N. forces in Korea. Meanwhile, the U.S. Army, Navy, Air Force and Marines arrived in Korea, and with the arrival of other U.N. troops from Great Britain, France, Canada, Australia and other countries, a counterattack was launched. The

Opposite: North Korean aggressors in Seoul with Russian tank.
Bottom : The U.N. Command is born. General Mac Arthur receives the U.N. flag.

Top: War refugees push on.
Middle: U.S. troops make a surprise-landing at Inchon
Bottom: Gen. MacArthur at the command post on the flag ship.

surprise-landing of the U.N. forces at Inchon on September 15 isolated North Korean troops in the south, and they were destroyed.

On September 28, Seoul was recovered, and under the authorization given by the U.N. and the U.S. government, U.S. and South Korean troops crossed the 38th parallel in pursuit of the fleeing North Korean troops. On October 19, the U.N. forces captured the North Korean capital of Pyongyang, and the U.N. forces reached the Yalu River on the western front and Chongjin on the eastern front.

The collapse of Communist North Korea was imminent, but in the middle of October over 150,000 Chinese Communist troops poured into Korea from Manchuria and an "entirely new war" in Korea began.

The U.N. forces withdrew from North Korea during the winter of 1950, and the Chinese and North Korean forces pushed southward across the 38th parallel, Seoul again being captured by the aggressors on January 4, 1951. However, the counterattack of the U.N. forces in March pushed back the aggressors beyond the 38th parallel, and a stalemate developed. The tide of the war gradually turned against North Korea.

The North Koreans proposed a truce through the Soviet Union, and talks began between the representatives of the two sides in the summer of 1951. But the truce talk progressed slowly. With the death of Joseph Stalin in early 1953 the North Koreans were anxious to end the war. As a result, the Korean Armistice was signed on July 27, 1953, and the four mile-wide demilitarized zone (DMZ) was established across the peninsula along the battle fronts. With this, the truce village of Panmunjom was put on the Korean map.

The North Korean ambition to conquer South Korea by force failed, but the war caused enormously heavy property damage in South Korea and no less than 2 million was casualties. Some two million North Koreans escaped to South Korea, fleeing from the Communists.

On 17 November 1954, the ROK and US bilateral peace treaty went into effect and since then the Theme "Partners in Peace" has become a reality as both nations have worked to maintain the peace. The price of this peace has been expensive as over 50 Americans and 500 South Koreans have given their lives due to North Korean hostile

acts since the signing of the Armistice.

Together these countries endured such brazen actions as two attempted assassinations of President Park Chung Hee, seizure of the *U.S.S. Pueblo*, sea borne infiltration attempts, the barbaric Panmunjom Axe Murder, and the downing of a US helicopter carrying supplies.

On May 22, 1982 proclamations were signed by President Chun Doo Hwan of Korea and President Ronald Reagan commemorating the centennial of the establishment of diplomatic relations between the two nations.

Top: *View of Panmunjom in 1950s.*
Middle: *POW during the truce negotiations.*
Bottom: *The truce was signed, but no peace was established.*

Right and opposite right: Returning POWs during operations Little Switch and Big Switch, 1953.
Bottom: A Military Armistice Commission meeting.

Bottom: "Hurrah! North Korea is the victor!" proclaims a North Korean propaganda monument erected in early 1953.

Left: The United Nations Honor Guard repatriate the remains of fallen soldiers in a full dress ceremony. On this day, 17 sets of remains were returned and flown to Hickom AFB, Hawaii, for identification (Jul. 12, 1993).

Bottom left: North Korean People's Army soldiers bring remains to the military

demarcation line for repatriation.
Right: Cameramen filming the repatriation of U.N. soldiers' remains during the 12 July 1993 repatriation. The bodies of 17 UNC soldiers who died during the Korean war returned.
Bottom: North Korean officers preparing for open casket inspections in front of Pan-mun-gak prior to repatriation by UN forces back (Jul. 12, 1993).

PUEBLO AFFAIR

Two days after a platoon of 31 commandos were intercepted in Seoul enroute to an attack on the ROK Presidential Mansion in an attempt to assassinate President Park Chung Hee, the North Korean navy hijacked the *U.S.S. Pueblo*. On 23 Jan 68 four armed NK patrol boats and 2 MIG jets captured the U.S. navy intelligence ship while in international waters twenty-five miles from the Korean coast. Six officers, 75 enlisted men, and two civilians were taken prisoners and forced to land at the NK port of Wonsan.

This was the first American ship to be seized in over 100 years and sparked graved concern in Congress. Rep. Bob Wilson (R-Calif) called it "Obviously an act of war." The Chairman of the Senate Armed Services Committee, Sen. Richard Russell (D-Ga) said "It was a very severe breach of international law that almost amounts to an act of war." Despite these concerns, the crew remained prisoners of war for eleven months until their release on 23 Dec 68. The release was made only after the Senior US Representative to the Military Armistice Commission, Major General Gilbert H. Woodward, signed a document stating that the *U.S.S. Pueblo* had illegally intruded into the territorial waters of North Korea. MG Woodward made it very clear to the free world that he signed the statement only to free the crew.

The 82 surviving crewmen and the remains of one seaman who died in captivity were returned to U.S. control, received a medical examination at the 121 Evacuation Hospital in Seoul, and then returned to San Diego for a Christmas Eve reunion with their families.

Opposite:UNC soldier inspecting 3rd Tunnel near Panmunjom.

Top : U.S.S. Peublo which was seized by North Korea on 23 January 1968.

Middle: Rites for 3 CH-47 Crewmen who were shot down when their helicopter strayed into North Korean airspace while delivering construction supplies to a ROK outpost near the eastern end of the DMZ. One survivor remained a prisoner of war for 57 hours.

Bottom: North Korean infiltration boat.

NORTH KOREA TUNNELS
THE DMZ

The 1st Tunnel (top) was discovered on 15 November 1974 at a distance 65 Km from Seoul. US Navy Commander Robert M. Ballinger was killed by an explosion while investigating this tun- Team. The North Korean government elected not to participate in this mission. The hall where tourists receive their briefing at Camp Bonifas to participate in this mission. The hall where tourists receive their briefing at Camp Kittyhawk prior to entering the DMZ is named in his memory.

The 2nd Tunnel (middle) was dug 1,100 meters south of the military demarcation line through solid granite 50 meters to 100 meters under the surface. This was discovered on 19 March 1975 near Chorwon, located 101 kilometers from Seoul.

On 17 October 1978 the 3rd infiltration (bottom) was discovered near Panmunjom. This tunnel, as well as the first two is directed toward Seoul. Approximately 30,000 armed troops accompanied by heavy guns and equipment could pass through this tunnel in one hour arriving at an exit point just 44 kilometers from Seoul. From this point they would be in a position to pin down UNC troops defending the DMZ, conduct rear area operations against the lines of supply in the Munsan corridor, or race to Seoul in less than one hour.

There may be 17 tunnels either completed or under construction at regular intervals along the DMZ. All tunnels were initiated in 1972 when the North opened a short-lived detente with the South. These tunnels are only one aspect of the militarization of the DMZ from 1953 to the present. While some of the fortifications, construction of mine field, and movement of artillery forward could be considered defensive, these tunnels have no other purpose than to mount a surprise attack against the Republic of Korea.

A RUSSIAN DEFECTS AT PANMUNJOM

Around 11:50 a.m. on November 23, 1984 a Russian who came to the Joint Security Area (JSA) at Panmunjom for sightseeing through the agency of North Korea took refuge in the United Nations Command (UNC) Security area, crossing the Military Demarcation Line (MDL).

North Korean guards in the JSA crossed into UNC jurisdiction in pursuit of this defector, shooting dead PFC Jang Myung Ki, a ROK soldier and injuring Pvt Michael A. Burgoryne, an American soldier.

17 North Korean guards crossed into shooting automatic rifles in pursuit of the Russian defector crossing the MDL, the UNC guards fired back, killing 3 North Korean guards and injuring 5.

The Russian defector was identified as Vasilly Matauzik, 22, a Russian translator.

Top right: A monument erected to the memory of the late PFC Jang Myung Ki killed while on guard.
Middle right: The UNC hands over the bodies of North Korean guards to the North Korea side.
Bottom right: A bird's-eye view of the JSA.
Bottom left: Two committeemen stand on Walking Bridge close by the quarters for Swedish and Swiss committee of the Neutral Nations Supervisory Commissions (NNSC). The North Korean guard post is on the other side of the bridge.

JANG BARRACKS

IN HONOR OF PFC JANG,MYUNG KI WHO WAS KILLED IN THE LINE OF DUTY BY KPA GUARDS WHILE PROTECTING THE LIVES OF HIS COMRADES AND A RUSSIAN DEFECTOR ON 23 NOVEMBER 1984.

29 NOV 1984

1984년 11월 23일 임무수행중 그의 동료와 쏘련 귀순자의 생명을 보호하다 북괴군 초병에 의해 전사한 일병 장명기를 추모하여 장막사라 명명함.

1984년 11월 29일

LOST RELATIVES FOUND

The photos here depict the efforts by the Korean Broadcasting System (KBS) to reunite families separated by the Korean War. During 5 months of live broadcasting in 1983 100,952 applications were submitted to KBS and 9,952 family members were reunited.

Upper left: Two old women are waiting endlessly for their separated family members.
Upper right: Two sisters reunited in 36 years are shedding tears of joy.
Bottom: They wrote on sheets of paper or cardboards the receipt numbers of KBS, particulars of themselves and their separated family members they're looking for; and posted them at Plaza of Reunion.

THE WAR IS NOT OVER

The 27 July 1953 Armistice Agreement did not end the Korean War. It only ended the fighting. Today the UNC continues to honor the spirit and intent of the Armistice as it represents itself at meetings in a professional manner, promptly and thoroughly investigates charges made by the North Koreans, and reports North Korean violations of the Armistice. On the other hand, North Korea has attempted to make Panmunjom a forum for its political propaganda, negotiate in a bombastic attitude as it refers to the UNC as US Imperialist Aggressors and the Chun Doo Hwan Puppet Government and has openly violated the provisions of the Armistice.

While the Armistice is not executed in the manner that was agreed to in July 1953, the Military Armistice Commissions meetings at JSA are a viable alternative to a shooting war. Peace is maintained through the constant efforts of the men who are:

"In Front of Them All."

Top: Christmas service at Aegi-bong hoping for reunification.
Bottom: Soldier inspecting fence along DMZ.

The Panmunjom Axe Murder

THE PANMUNJOM AXE MURDER

The Panmunjom Axe Murder occurred at approximately 11:00 a.m. on 18 August 1976. A UNC work force was to prune a poplar tree which was located approximately 50 meters from UNC 3 and 75 meters east of the Bridge of No Return. The tree needed to be trimmed as it blocked the view between OP5 and UNC 3. The guard at UNC 3 is adjacent to the Military Demarcation Line and has called his post the "Loneliest Place in the World." There needed to be unimpared vision between OP 5 and UNC 3. In fact, the trimming of trees, cutting of trees, cleaning brush, etc., is considered routine work at the JSA and had been accomplished over the years by both sides without serious incident. Although the poplar tree was clearly on the southern side of the MDL, it was next to the road the KPA guards used to enter and exit the JSA. The KPA would enter the JSA

by crossing the Bridge of No Return, passing by UNC Checkpoint 3, and turn left just past the tree on their way to their work area. Later on the KPA would state that the poplar tree was a tree that was planted and nurtured by the North Koreans.

On 6 August 4 UNC guards and 6 Korean Service Corps workers began to accomplish their routine task. A KPA guard questioned them and told them to leave the tree alone. However, the KPA did not lodge a protest nor call for an immediate on-the-spot security officer's meeting to protest as is the usual custom. Since the KPA had shown an interest in the tree the JSA commander took several additional precautions before proceeding with the work. He organized a 10 man security force, stationed the rest of the duty platoon at UNC 4 as a quick reaction force, placed additional guards and cameras at OP 5 and UNC 3, designated a foreman to supervise the Korean

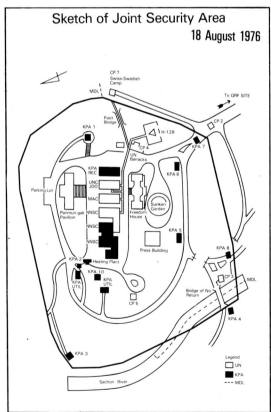

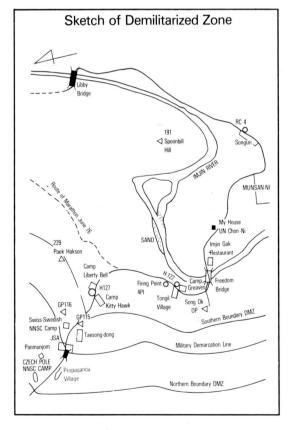

Service Corps workers, and directed the on-scene, commander to request an on-the-spot security officer's meeting should a confrontation occur.

At 10:30 hours on 18 August 1976 the UNC work party arrived at the tree to begin their work. Within a minute or so a KPA Lieutenant and 9 guards arrived and were briefed on the task. The work began without incident. However at approximately 10:50 the KPA lieutenant demanded that the work stop. The officer in charge, Captain Bonifas, directed the workers to continue since this was a legitimate activity and the work needed to be accomplished.

The KPA lieutenant dispatched a runner to get reinforcements. By 11:00 the number of KPA guards had grown to approximately 30. The KPA officer again ordered the work to stop. When the work continued, he removed his watch, wrapped it in a handkerchief, placed it in his pocket and yelled "Kill the Americans."

The targets of the attack were the two American officers as they were pounced upon immediately.

The axes brought in by the work force were savagely used by the KPA during the fight. The fight lasted only 4 minutes. The momentum of the attack was disrupted when the driver of the 2½ ton truck pulled his truck forward to protect the already mutilated body of Captain Bonifas from further assault. This movement was enough the cause the North Koreans to break off the attack and scramble to safety across the Bridge of No Return. However, Captain Bonifas (Posthumously promoted to major) and Lieutenant Barrett were slain while 4 US enlisted men and 4 ROK soldiers were injured. KPA casualties are still unknown; however, at a later meeting the KPA claimed five of their soldiers were injured. The world waited to see what would happen in this corner of the world on the edge of freedom.

The fight begins. Arrow highlights North Korean soldiers (KPA) surrounding Captain Bonifas.

A sequence of events (from left to right) showing steps leading to and the Panmunjom Axe Murder. Some of the arrows highlight North Korean atrocities.

OPERATION PAUL BUNYAN

For three days that tree stood as a challenge to free men everywhere. Immediately after the fight, the Quick Reaction Forces of the JSA and of the 2nd Bn, 9th Infantry (Manchu) were ready for immediate deployment. A UNC crisis action team was formed in Yongsan. General Richard Stilwell, the CINC, who was visiting Japan, immediately returned to Korea. Across the entire peninsula troops increased their readiness as planners developed what would be known as OPERATION PAUL BUNYAN.

The foremost American in the field of tree-cutting was the legendary Paul Bunyan, who cut down eighty-one trees with one swipe of his mighty ax. There are many tales of Paul Bunyan and his great blue ox, Babe, that are told in lumber camps in the United States. Together, this team dug the St. Lawrence River and cut down the trees from the Mississippi River to the Rockies, thereby creating the Great Plains. When the chain saw and locomotive replaced this great wood-cutting team, Paul Bunyan and Babe moved on the Alaska and still create the aurora borealis, the lights that brighten the Northern Hemisphere, by their wrestling matches. It was appropriate then that the name of this operation to cut down the poplar tree be codenamed OPERATION PAUL BUNYAN.

The UNC plan was developed to establish the right of movement in the JSA, to remove the tree from the JSA, and to generate sufficient combat power to accomplish the mission.

The burden of cutting down the tree fell on the shoulders of the 2nd Engineer Battalion, and more specifically, the men of Company B, which supported the Western Corridor. The Commander of the United Nations Command Security Force, Joint Security Area, would control all actions in Panmunjom and the 2nd Battalion 9th Infantry (Manchu) would provide the security.

US Engineers at the tree protected by ROKA Special Forces and JSA Security Force Soldiers.

As the planners from the US 2nd Infantry Division and JSA were developing courses of action, US Air Force and Naval units were ordered to Korea. The *U.S.S. Midway* was ordered to proceed to an operational area in the southern straights of South Korea. F-11S, from Mountain Home Air Force Base, Idaho were alerted, scrambled, refueled over the Pacific Ocean, and were in Korea within a 20 hour period. F-4's from Okinawa, and two B-52's increased the combat power.

The men of the 2nd Battalion 9th Infantry (Manchu) knew something was going to happen. On 5 August the battalion went on alert because of a machine gun firing incident on the DMZ. A day earlier had been started with an early morning alert to initiate the 3rd Brigade Command Post Exercise. Because this was the third alert in one month when the normal rate is one or two and because minutes later after the alert sirens sounded a medical evacuation helicopter landed momentarily at Camp Greaves enroute to the 121 Medical Evacuation Hospital at Seoul, the soldiers knew this was more than a training exercise. When the live ammunition, to include TOW rounds (anti-tank weapons capable of defeating armor) were distributed in accordance with the company supply plans, each soldier knew that this was for real and that his unit was going in.

Simultaneously a tank heavy team was formed at Camp Casey ready to reduce Panmunjom to a parking lot if necessary to accomplish the mission. The 2nd Aviation Battalion Commander planned how he would support this operation with Cobra attack helicopters and 20 Huey helicopters. The engineers planned to cut the tree and were assigned three other missions: be prepared to perform demolition guard duties on Freedom Bridge, destroy the illegal roadblocks placed in the southern portion of JSA by the KPA, and be prepared to conduct a hasty river crossing to evacuate soldiers south across the Imjin River.

Two limbs down, one to go.

JSA soldiers, infantrymen, engineers, helicopter pilots, mechanics, artillerymen, and other support personnel planned and rehearsed their plans, checked and double-checked from their alert until the first truck crossed the start point.

The operation that unfolded at 07:00 hrs Saturday morning 21 August 1976 paralleled the plan. Reveille was 04:00 for the 1st ROK Infantry Division Recon Company and at 04:30 hours for all other soldiers in Task Force Vierra, the unit charged with cutting the tree. At 05:00 sirens sounded throughout the 2nd Infantry Division area placing their units on alert and scrambling soldiers to their vehicles for immediate action. By 06:30 all ground forces in Task Force Vierra were ready to enter the DMZ and 15 minutes later twenty UH-1 Hueys supported by 8 Cobra gunships were ready to support the operation.

At 06:45 the Task Force Commander, LTC Vierra gave a message to the Joint Duty Officer to be handed to the KPA counterpart which read:

"At 07:00 hours a United Nations Command work force will enter the Joint Security Area to complete the task begun on Wednesday. Should there be no interference the work will be completed and the work force will leave." Three minutes later the first element moved out.

Twelve minutes later at 07:00 hours the Task Force had entered the JSA and moved directly to the tree. The engineers began to trim the tree one limb at a time. 64 ROK Special Force soldiers formed a ring around the tree as the first line of defense. These soldiers were all blackbelts in Tae Kwon Do or Judo and President Park Chung Hee committed these warriors with the statement that "if the North Koreans show up with their weapons, these soldiers could disarm and beat them with their own weapons." One JSA Security Platoon had moved into position armed with pick ax handles. The 1953 Armistice Agreement limited the number of weapons in the JSA and the UNC lived by the agreement. The first element with

The tree is down, let's move out.

weapons was the Reconnaissance Company of the 1st Infantry Division which was located just outside of the Joint Security Area in a woodline where they could support the operation. One minute away by air were 140 soldiers from Bravo and Charlie Companies 2nd Bn 9th Infantry (Manchu) who were ready to add their firepower if needed. One truck was parked at the eastern end of the Bridge of No Return to block any KPA effort to interfere with the tree cutting.

The 30 year old Normandy Poplar was cut about 9 feet above ground where the three large limbs branched out. By 07:18 the first limb of the tree was cut off. Simultaneous to the tree cutting operation other engineers moved to destroy the illegal KPA road blocks installed in the southern portion of JSA. An engineer 5 ton truck hooked a chain from the truck to the illegal barrier and started pulling. The first barrier was pulled out slightly after the first limb had fallen.

Poplar trees are very sappy and the operators had a difficult time cutting through the branches as each chain saw would be gummed up. In addition it was almost impossible to get the proper cutting angle to prevent the limb from bearing down on the saw. In all, 13 chain saws were used and the final limb was felled as the engineers formed a human chain, holding on to each side of their platoon leader, 1st Lieutenant G. L. Deason, who finished the operation at 07:45 hours, 15 minutes after all the illegal barriers were pulled out.

Within 45 minutes upon entering the JSA the Task Force had removed the illegal barriers and completed the tree cutting mission initiated earlier that week. Once the mission had been accomplished the ROKA Special Forces soldiers, US and ROK Engineers and Infantrymen, and the JSA forces left the area, leaving only the stump to remind all who would visit Panmunjom the resolve of the UNC to maintain freedom in the Republic of Korea.

The tree is down and all are out of JSA.

MILITARY ARMISTICE COMMISSION MEETING

As the UNC crisis action team was developing courses of action and as the combat soldiers were preparing for any possible mission, the Military Armistice Commission had called for the 379th Meeting to discuss this matter in proper channels. The meeting was initially called to convene in the morning of the 19th of August. A North Korean counter-offer of meeting at 16:00 hours was accepted. The Senior Member of the UNC passed a protest to the KPA representative regarding the murder of the two American officers and requested that the message which demanded a North Korean apology and retribution to the families of the dead officers be given to Kim Il Sung.

During this meeting the North Korean Senior Representative attempted to shift the blame for the Panmunjom Axe Murder to the UNC as he explained that the deadly axes carried by the work force were brought into the JSA in violation of the Armistice. When that effort failed, he attempted to discuss other alleged violations. The UNC was resolved to discuss only the Panmunjom Axe Murder and related facts. The meeting lasted one hour and 40 minutes with no solution reached at the conference table.

Immediately after OPERATION PAUL BUNYAN the KPA Senior Member requested a meeting with the UNC to answer the message presented on 19 August 1976. The North Koreans regretted that the incident occurred. While not a direct apology, the word regretful as used in the message was significant for it is as close as the North Koreans would ever come to an admission of guilt. The response was also unique in that it was devoid of the unusual rhetoric that is used by the North Koreans in meetings. In one meeting the United States was referred to as the U.S. Imperialist Aggressor more than 300 times.

At 16:00 hours 25 August 1976 the 380th MAC

One of the daily meetings of the Joint Observer Team.

meeting convened as the UNC acknowledged the KPA message delivered immediately after OPERATION PAUL BUNYAN. The UNC informed the KPA that their message was unsatisfactory and requested that immediate assurances be given that the safety of UNC personnel in the JSA be preserved, that orders guaranteeing their safety be issued to all KPA personnel and that those guards responsible for the murder of the two UNC officers be punished. The KPA proposed that the MDL be used as the line to physically separate military personnel. The meeting concluded with no agreements.

Three days later the 381st MAC Meeting convened. During this meeting the UNC again requested assurances for the safety of the UNC personnel and removal of the four KPA guard posts south of the MDL. After studying the results of the meeting the UNC determined that they had extracted all the assurances for the safety of UNC personnel that the KPA could be expected to give, that the UNC would not receive any further apology, and because the UNC had no guard posts north of the MDL, the KPA agreement to remove their four guard posts south of the MDL was a clear concession. The UNC believed the time had come to defuse the meetings and referred future negotiations to the Secretaries.

The 446th Secretary's Meeting was convened on 31 August 1976 and details negotiations continued for six sessions concluding on 6 September 1976. Out of these negotiations came the requirement to form a Joint Survey to redefine the MDL.

The Joint Observer Team met daily during the period 7 to 22 September to implement the provisions of the agreement negotiated by the Secretaries. By defining and marking the MDL a separation of the security forces of each side could be assured and the probability of confrontation within the JSA is reduced.

Military Armistice Commission Meeting.

EPILOGUE OF AXE MURDER INCIDENT

By 16 September 1976 the work to remark the MDL and remove the four KPA guard posts had been completed. In the outer regions 10cm × 10cm × 1 meter high concrete posts, spaced 10 meters apart, were placed between each of the original MDL markers to clearly identify the line. A 50cm wide × 5cm high concrete pavement was poured between all the Military Armistice Commission Buildings and extends 10 meters on both the east and west side of the buildings. Engineers and work parties from both sides constructed the markers and poured concrete to mark their respective portions of the MDL.

Meanwhile KPA personnel removed the four guard posts on the UNC side of the MDL.

With the work complete and the MDL defined, members of the opposing sides are restrained from entering the other side's buildings and crossing the MDL except under very strict conditions.

In order to accomplish this the KPA were compelled to find a different entrance to the JSA as their customary route carried them across the Bridge of No Return into South Korea enroute to their place of duty north of the MDL. A second bridge was constructed in 72 hours to enable the KPA guards to enter JSA without violating the new agreement. The major exception to this restricted movement is in the Military Armistice Commission Building and the Neutral National Supervisory Buildings where free movement is permitted.

The North Korean government had received a political black eye during this incident and was humiliated as it merely observed the UNC Task Force cut down the internationally famous tree and remove the illegal road barriers that had been in place since 1965. Apparently the north perceived it to be in their best interest to resolve the matter quickly and that the risk of further confrontation or provocation was too high and even greater loss of prestige was probable.

The determination and resolve demonstrated

Engineers pouring concrete.

by the soldiers, sailors, and airmen of OPERA-TION PAUL BUNYAN earned the respect of entire world. Their willingness to take the necessary risks and to perform their duty in a professional matter enabled the UNC to reestablish its rights of movement in the JSA. The division of the Joint Security Area was designed to prevent further incident inside of the boundary of this explosive site. A year after the Axe Murder a US CH-47 helicopter carrying construction supplies was shot down when it strayed over the MDL in eastern Korea. In 1978 the 3rd Infiltration Tunnel was discovered. It was less than a decade later when another serious incident happened at Panmunjom despite the separation between the opposing forces. On 23 November 1984 a Russian who was touring Panmunjom on a North Korean sponsored tour bolted from his group and ran to freedom in the south. 20 to 30 KPA guards opened fire and ran across the MDL in an effort to prevent the defection. The quick thinking of the UNC guards on duty saved the life of the defector, but the

gunfire exchange resulted in the death of one Republic of Korea soldier and three KPA guards.

Lt. General Maxwell D. Taylor, Commanding General Eighth United States Army on the occasion of the 27 July 1953 Armistice signing stated:

"There is no occasion for celebration or boisterous conduct. We are faced with the same enemy, only a short distance away, and must be ready for any move he makes."

These words are as appropriate today as they were in 1953.

Today all soldiers on the "Frontier of Freedom" are performing their duties in a professional manner and are prepared for any unpredictable action. Despite all the provocations to war by the north since 1953, the peninsula is at peace. The efforts of the Republic of Korea and United States forces will maintain this peace and keep the Armistice in effect until the Korean War is finally ended.

Joint Observer Team between buildings.

TO MEMORIALIZE

    Major Arthur G. Bonifas and 1Lt. Mark T. Barrett killed in action, 18 August 1976, Panmunjom, Korea. Their hats represent their everlasting presence for duty in this unit. Their badges, never to be worn again, rest here in recognition of the vigil these two soldiers keep, even in death. This wood, a piece of tree that no longer stands commemorate the resolve of two nations and courage of a few soldiers, who will always remember, who can never forget, but who must not look back.

BADGE # 9 Maj. Bonifas "Bonifas"
BADGE #12 1Lt. Barrett "Big Bear"

Memorial located in the "Monastery," Camp Bonifas.

A New Era of Reconciliation

SOUTH-NORTH RED CROSS CONFERENCES

After years of preparation that began in the 1970s amid anticipation and excite-ment, the South-North Korean Red Cross Conferences were held in 1985 in Seoul and Pyongyang in a festive mood. But despite the South Korean Red Cross' efforts to bring separated families together as soon as possible, procedures for the talks were often disrupted, due to the North's attempts to use the conferences for political propaganda.

Top: North Korean Red Cross delegates' long-awaited encounter with their separated families in Seoul (Sep. 29, 1985).

Bottom: South and North Korean chief delegates pose for photographers at a main conference session (Dec. 3, 1985).

Top right: North Korean Red Cross delegates cross the border to the South through Freedom House (Sep. 20, 1985).
Middle right: Bishop Chi Hak-sun and other South Korean delegates finally arrive in Pyongyang in hopes of visiting their homeland in the North for the first time in 40 years (Sep. 20, 1985).
Upper left: Bishop Chi Hak-sun and his younger sister are in tears at their reunion in Pyongyang (Sep. 21, 1985).
Bottom: Rice sent from the North for South Korean flood victims is being transported to Taesong-ni.

SOUTH-NORTH PREMIERS' TALKS

The 1st South-North Premiers' Talks were held in Seoul for three days in September of 1992 with eight delegates from each side participating, headed by South Korean premier Kang Young-hoon and Premier Yon Hyong-muk from the North.

After a series of talks that followed in both Seoul and Pyongyang, the historical "Reconciliation and Non-aggression Pact Between South and North was signed on Dec. 13, 1991 at the 5th conference. The agreement opened a whole new era of peaceful co-existence of the two sides after 46 years of division. The pact, comprised of 4 chapters and 25 articles on politics, arms, economy and reunions of separated families, is expected to stay in effect until reunification.

Previously in the 1970s, the South-North Coordinating Committee had been held in an attempt to open talks between the two sides, headed by Lee Hu-rak of South Korea and Park Song-chol of the North.

The premiers of the South and North shake hands after signing the historical non-aggression pact on Dec. 13, 1991.

Upper left: In 1972, Park Chung-hee receives a visit from Park Song-chol, North Korean vice-premier who has arrived in Seoul secretly.
Upper right: North Korean Premier Yon Hyong-muk is greeted by South Korean President Roh Tae-woo at Chongwadae.
Bottom left: The premiers of the South and

North shake hands after signing the historical non-aggression pact on Dec. 13, 1991.
Bottom right: Lee Hu-rak, South Korean chairman to the South-North Coordinating Committee is headed across the border for talks in Pyongyang (March 14, 1973).

CULTURAL EXCHANGE BETWEEN SOUTH AND NORTH

The "Pan-National Reunification Music Festival" was held in Pyongyang on Oct. 18, 1990 as the first attempt in cultural exchange between the two divided nations. Seventeen delegates from the South Korean National Artists Alliance crossed the border through Panmunjom and were warmly received at the festival.

On Dec. 18 of the same year, the Seoul Traditional Music and Dance Troupe invited North Korean musicians to the "'90 Year-End Reunification Traditional Music Festival." Thirty-three North Korean delegates participated in the festival.

Southern musicians are introduced first at the "Pan-National Reunification Music Festival" held in Pyongyang (Oct. 18, 1990).

North Korean citizens greet Southern delegates to the "Pan-National Reunification Music Festival" at Panmunjom (Oct. 14, 1990).

Top, middle right: North Korean musicians and
ancers perform at the "'90 Year-End Reunification Traditional Music Festival" in Seoul
(Dec. 8, 1990).
Upper left: South Korean delegates performing a traditional dance (Dec. 8, 1990).
Bottom: North Korean delegates make a cur-
tain call after their Seoul performance (Dec. 8,
1990).

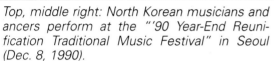

SOUTH-NORTH SPORTS EXCHANGE

Ever since the 1st South-North Sports Talks were held on Nov. 29, 1990 in Panmunjom, consistent effort from both sides helped subsequent talks to develop, resulting in the historical agreement to send a South-North unified team to the 41st World Table Tennis Championships in 1991. The single-team participation was successful, not only in the fruitful results at the games but also in fostering a strong feeling of national identity for the players and those who cheered at home.

Another unified team was organized for the 6th World Junior Soccer Championships and the team held practice matches in Seoul and Pyongyang, bringing the dream of reunification closer for all Koreans.

Chairman of the Korean Olympic Committee Kim Taek-soo (on the left) shakes hands with Oh Hyon-joo, the head of North Korean Olympic team just after they signed an agreement on South-North sports exchanges.

South-North unified women's soccer team pose for photographers after their practice match at the Olympic Stadium in Seoul (May 8, 1991).

INTER-KOREAN TRADE

Until recently, trade between South and North was exchanged indirectly through third nations. But attempts are now being made for direct inter-Korean trade: In 1991, South Korean rice was shippd from Mokpo to the North Korean port of Najin, and in 1992 North Korean-manufactured clothing went on sale at a Seoul department store.

With the plans for the Nampo Special Trade Zone and the Tumen River Trade Zone being developed, exchange between South and North Korean businessmen are increasing. Anticipation runs high that it won't be long before joint ventures between South Korean technology and North Korean manpower are introduced on the international market.

Top: North Korean delegates visit Samsung Electronics Co. in Suwon, showing their interests in the modernized production facilities and goods.
Upper left: Reunification Rice is shipped on to Condor at Mokpo, headed for Najin port in the North (July 1991).
Bottom left: A North Korean product exhibition in Seoul.
Bottom right: Mokpo citizens cheer Condor as she sets sail.